CELTIC

THIRD EDITION

Edited by **GRAHAM McCOLL**

CARLTON
BOOKS

THE LITTLE BOOK OF CELTIC

THIRD EDITION

This edition published in 2012
First published by Carlton Books in 2004

A CIP catalogue record for this book is available
from the British Library.

ISBN 978-1-84732-939-4

Printed in China

INTRODUCTION

The boisterousness and passions that surround Celtic ensure that there is always plenty to be said about the club. Great players, off-field intrigues and masterful managers have inspired many words of wisdom and wit to be uttered about Celtic down the years and many of those words have landed on these pages.

Great games also demand exceptional explanations and Celtic have participated in many of the most historic matches in the history of football; none greater than the 1967 European Cup final, when they became the first British club to win the European Cup. That game and other massive Celtic matches are encapsulated in the pithy and precise words that such occasions often bring out of those who were involved.

The quotes on these pages are reflections of Celtic, a special club, in all its colour, variety and fun. They will raise many smiles and memories for every Celtic fan…

"The Greatest Team on Earth. "

Local billing for Celtic on a visit to the Midlands during the 1890s

" I was told when I joined about Celtic's "paranoia". Now I know it is true. We are hard done by. Religiously and politically, there are people against us. **"**

Liam Brady, *Celtic manager, October 1992*

> **"** Even when we played the likes of Raith Rovers or Dunfermline, the referees would be against us. That's because in Scotland it's always a two-horse race and, by hurting us, they were helping Rangers. **"**

Paolo Di Canio, *2000*

We knew they'd lie down and they have done.

Chris Sutton *on Dunfermline Athletic, after the Fife club had lost 6–1 to Rangers at Ibrox on 25 May 2003. That result meant Rangers took the 2002–03 Premier League title by a margin of one on goal difference over Celtic*

> **"** I'm a bit of a dreamer but I'm also a realist. I've got a three-year contract and I want to do things relatively quickly. I might get a little bit of time at the start but that won't last forever. I know the pitfalls. **"**

Martin O'Neill *on his appointment as Celtic manager, June 2000*

66 The game was 90 minutes long but for me the game lasted as long as my five years as captain and our six years without a trophy. **99**

Paul McStay, *in 1995, on the 1–0 Scottish Cup final victory over Airdrie that brought Celtic their first trophy of the 1990s*

66 The operation was a success but the patient died on the table. **99**

Ebbe Skovdahl, *Aberdeen manager, after a defensive Aberdeen side had lost to two late goals in a 2–0 defeat to Celtic at Celtic Park, September 2001*

> **One of my jobs at the start – and you can write this as a headline – was trying to find out exactly why we had spent some of our money on Rafael Scheidt.** "

Martin O'Neill, *in September 2004, recalls taking over as Celtic manager in 2000. Scheidt, a Brazilian centre-back signed by John Barnes for £5 million from Corinthians, played just six games for Celtic*

66 They spot talent others seem to be unaware of; they know what the team needs and how and where to buy replacements without always having to pay a fortune; and they get the best out of the squad they've assembled. 99

Brian Clough *on his former players John Robertson and Martin O'Neill, 2002*

66 You can't have one man in a club saying, "I am Celtic FC." This is a team effort and everyone is part of it. This League title was not won in one year or by one man. **99**

Fergus McCann, *Celtic's managing director, after Wim Jansen had resigned as Celtic's head coach two days after leading the club to its first championship in ten years, May 1998*

" I know there are head coaches here and there now but I can't get used to that terminology. I am a manager and I want to be involved in everything. That way, if things go wrong, then my neck is on the block and if things go well I get the acclaim. **"**

Martin O'Neill, *2002*

66 We thought it would be impossible. We had seen Real Madrid and all those teams play, the Milans and all those, and they had looked magnificent. **99**

Bobby Lennox, *in 2003, on the players' assessment of their chances of winning the European Cup at the start of the 1966–67 season*

66 We knew, within ourselves, our own ability and we started to believe in ourselves but we never, ever, thought for one minute that we would win the European Cup. **99**

Jimmy Johnstone, *1995*

" At that point we had no thoughts of winning the European Cup. In fact, it was a big thrill for us just to go to Zurich because we had never been there. **"**

Bobby Lennox, *in 2003, on Celtic's opening European Cup tie with the Swiss champions in September 1966*

❝ I feel we have the players fit to wear the mantle of champions of Europe, I have told them so. Now they know it's up to them. **❞**

Jock Stein *before the second leg of Celtic's European Cup quarter-final with Vojvodina Novi Sad, March 1967*

66 We thought that we could beat them. I thought that that Celtic team could have beaten anybody on the right day. 99

Bobby Lennox, *in 2003, on Celtic's attitude to the 1967 European Cup final with Inter Milan*

❝ I thought we were going to get a doing. They were the best defensive side in the world. **❞**

Jimmy Johnstone, *in 1995, on his feelings prior to facing Inter*

66 There wasn't a side in the world could afford to give us as much of the ball as they did without being beaten. We had nine potential goal-scorers and they gave us the ball. **99**

Tommy Gemmell *on the 1967 European Cup final with ultra-defensive Inter*

66 After the first 20 minutes I was thinking, "Are these guys kidding us on? When are they going to start to play?" Because we were running them ragged. We could have beaten them 10–0. **99**

Jimmy Johnstone *on the final with Inter*

66 As soon as I scored that goal, the Italian players' heads went down. They didn't want to know after that. They knew the writing was on the wall. **99**

Tommy Gemmell *on his equaliser to make it 1–1 in the 63rd minute of the 1967 European Cup final*

66 A defender came to me and then another defender went behind him. I just did the wee Ali-shuffle and knocked it back to Bobby Murdoch who had a shot at goal, which was going past, and Stevie slid it into the net. We did exactly the same thing in training every day of the week. **99**

Tommy Gemmell *on Stevie Chalmers' goal which made it 2–1 in the 1967 European Cup final and ultimately clinched the trophy for Celtic*

66 It was about 75 degrees: it would have burned a hole in your head. We didn't even think about that because when we got the ball we wanted to run and run and skin them. 99

Jimmy Johnstone *on the 1967 European Cup final*

66 We can have no complaints. Celtic deserved their victory. We were beaten by Celtic's force. Although we lost, the match was a victory for sport. **99**

Helenio Herrera, *the Inter manager, after Celtic's 2–1 victory in the National Stadium, Lisbon*

66 We won and we won on merit.
This win gives us more satisfaction
than anything. I can still hardly
believe it's true. **99**

Jock Stein *moments after Celtic's
famous victory*

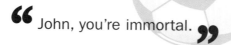

66 John, you're immortal. **99**

Bill Shankly, *Liverpool manager, to Jock Stein
following Celtic's great achievement*

66 You could take all the derby matches in the world, add them all together and they still wouldn't equal one-millionth of the Old Firm. There is nothing like it. **99**

Paolo Di Canio, *2000*

" I asked the team to go out and climb a mountain. When they got to the top, they found there was another hill to scale. They did it marvellously. "

Billy McNeill *on Celtic's dramatic 4–2 victory over Rangers to take the 1978–79 League title, May 1979*

" I only know the first two lines of "The Sash" because after that we've usually scored. **"**

Roy Aitken, *captain of Celtic, on matches with Rangers in the 1980s*

66 There was hatred in the Old Firm and I soaked it up. I used it to my advantage. I knew perfectly well that it was about religion and, while I did not understand or wish to get involved in the dispute, I would feed off it. **99**

Paolo Di Canio, *2000*

66 During the first half hour we possibly played the best football I have ever seen in an Old Firm match. **99**

Billy McNeill, *Celtic manager, on the 1–0 victory over Rangers, August 1987*

When the final whistle blows and you're in front; that's the only moment when you really enjoy it.

Martin O'Neill *on Old Firm matches, August 2004*

❝ I've always seen us as the Cavaliers and them as the Roundheads. **❞**

Billy McNeill *on*
Celtic and Rangers, 1988

❝ I'm often asked how this Rangers team compares with the Lisbon Lions. I have to be honest and say I think it would be a draw but, then, some of us are getting on for 60. **❞**

Bertie Auld, *in 1993, after Rangers had reached the group stage of the Champions League for the first time*

" It's not that they weren't penalties – it's just that they're the kind of penalties that nobody else gets! **"**

Not The View, *Celtic fanzine, after Rangers were awarded three penalties in their 2–2 draw at Dundee, May 2003*

66 Celtic and Rangers are fantastic football clubs, great clubs, who stand still in their environment because of money. **99**

Martin O'Neill, *after Celtic's 3–1 home Champions League defeat by Barcelona, September 2004*

It is scary. The hatred you encounter in some grounds is just frightening, especially when you see a grown man standing next to a kid and throwing verbal abuse at you. It does sicken me.

Henrik Larsson *comments on sectarian and racial abuse in Scottish football, May 2004*

> **"** They never die who live in the hearts of those they leave behind. **"**

Memorial card for John Thomson, the Celtic goalkeeper who suffered a fatal blow to the head in a match with Rangers, September 1931

He was law, he was the boss; an iron-fisted man.

Johnnie Wilson, *Celtic player of the 1930s, speaking in 2002, on Willie Maley, manager of Celtic from 1897 to 1940*

66 Even if something had gone wrong on a Saturday and a player had made an obvious mistake, McGrory would never come across and speak to the guy during the week. We never got an ounce of coaching from either McStay or McGrory. **99**

Alec Boden, *ex-Celt, in 2002, on Jimmy McStay, Celtic manager 1940–45, and Jimmy McGrory, manager 1945–65*

66 I've got a vivid memory from 1965, when it was announced that he was coming back from Hibs, of Billy McNeill saying, "Oh, that's fantastic. Wait and see how things change now." 99

John Divers, *in 1995, on the return as Celtic manager of Jock Stein, former Celtic coach and player*

66 It is up to us, to everyone at Celtic Park, to build up our own legends. We don't want to live with history, to be compared with legends from the past. We must make new legends. **99**

Jock Stein, *after winning his first League championship with Celtic, May 1966*

66 He would confront people. He would have a square-go if it was on. He was a big, strong guy; quite a fearsome character. **99**

Alastair Hunter, *Celtic goalkeeper of Jock Stein, 2002*

❝ You knew, going out there, what to do and what your team-mates had to do and invariably he gave you the feeling that if you did it properly you would win. Normally, that was the case. **❞**

David Hay, *in 1995, on Jock Stein, Celtic manager from 1965 to 1978*

> **"** When the Rangers game came round, for instance, and they were going to give you £1000 if you won, that was a driving force to get players to play. If you were on £55 a week and had the chance to earn £1000, you would kill, wouldn't you? **"**

Lou Macari *on Celtic's bonus scheme in the 1970s under Jock Stein*

66 He got the best out of me individually and within the system of the team. Accordingly, he got the best out of the team. **99**

David Hay *on Jock Stein, 2002*

" He was good at training; he kept your interest in it. You weren't slogging about doing boring things. You were always working with a ball. "

Alastair Hunter *on Jock Stein*

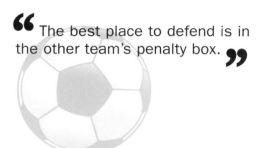

66 The best place to defend is in the other team's penalty box. **99**

Jock Stein

We like Scotland because we love shortbread. Coming here is interesting to him.

Nivaldo Baldo, *advisor to Celtic trialist Marcio Amoroso, a Brazilian, 2004*

66 How dare Martin O'Neill ask Rivaldo to go for a trial in America! That is an insult to my client and to football. People will be crying tears of laughter when they hear Celtic wanted to take Rivaldo on trial. **99**

Carlos Arime, *Rivaldo's agent, June 2004*

"We'll fit him in somewhere."

Martin O'Neill *on the question of how to accommodate Juninho in the Celtic team after the Brazilian became the first World Cup-medal winner to sign for the club, August 2004*

66 Scoring the goal that gets your team through to a major cup final is the sort of thing you dream about as a kid. **99**

Henrik Larsson *after scoring the goal against Boavista that took Celtic into the UEFA Cup final, April 2003*

66 Ronaldinho, watch out! **99**

Martin O'Neill *on Aiden McGeady, after the 18-year-old's debut, April 2004*

66 I just kept my head down and tried to hit it low. I looked up, saw it hit the inside of the post and then the back of the net. It was a bit of a shock really, when I saw it hit the back of the net. It was a good goal, actually. **99**

Aiden McGeady *after scoring on his debut for Celtic, away to Heart of Midlothian, 2004*

" We didn't get swapping our jerseys in those days. We only had two sets of jerseys – one set would be getting cleaned and we would be wearing the other set. **"**

Bobby Carroll, *in 2003, on being unable to exchange jerseys with Ferenc Puskas after Celtic's friendly match with Real Madrid in September 1962*

66 Without a shadow of a doubt that was my best game for Celtic. With a quarter of an hour to go, none of them would come near me. **99**

Jimmy Johnstone, *in 1995, on teasing Real Madrid's defence in Celtic's 1–0 victory in Alfredo di Stefano's testimonial match, 1967*

" The Johnstone display equalled, and probably bettered, the best performance I have seen from any other player in the world. **"**

Jock Stein *after Jimmy Johnstone had excelled in Celtic's 5–1 European Cup victory over Red Star Belgrade, 1968*

❝ I hit the ball against the goalkeeper. It was just one of those things but I reckon that, when I did that, that was me finished at Celtic. Jock Stein was like that: he tended to blame you for things. Within a year I had left the club. **❞**

John Hughes *on missing a goalscoring chance at 1–1 in extra-time against Feyenoord in the 1970 European Cup final*

66 It will stick in my mind for ever that after the game the Celtic players were extremely good sportsmen and, together with their supporters, they gave us a standing ovation when we were receiving the cup. **99**

Eddy Pieters Graafland, *the Feyenoord goalkeeper, on Feyenoord's 2–1 victory over Celtic in the 1970 European Cup final*

❝ If someone says to me, "What about that goal you scored in the European Cup final?" invariably they are talking about Lisbon and 1967. No one ever mentions the goal I scored against Feyenoord. It just shows you: when you are losers no one wants to know. When you are winners, everybody wants to know. **❞**

Tommy Gemmell, *1995*

"There was just this deadly silence on the bus going back to our hotel. It was as if the whole world had collapsed. Nobody spoke. **"**

Evan Williams, *in 2003, on the aftermath of Celtic's 2–1 defeat by Feyenoord in the 1970 European Cup final*

66 That defeat in the 1970 European Cup final took a lot out of the club and took a lot out of the self-belief and everything else. We never, ever quite got to that level again. **99**

Billy McNeill, *1998*

66 We thought they were on something! **99**

John Hughes, *in 2003, on facing an energetic Ajax side, European champions elect, in the European Cup, 1971*

❝ I think Celtic are as good as the best teams here in Italy. **❞**

Carlo Ancelloti, *Milan head coach, piles on the flattery in advance of Celtic's Champions League match in Milan, September 2004*

66 Right through my career
I have dreamed of the day
I might be offered the job
as Celtic manager. **99**

Billy McNeill, *on being appointed successor to Jock
Stein as Celtic manager, May 1978*

66 How could my players get injured the way they played? If anyone is injured then he must have fallen coming out of the bath. **99**

Billy McNeill, *faces up to the realities of being Celtic manager after a 2–0 loss at Hearts in October 1978*

66 The best player of them all for me was Paul McStay. He was like the bandleader; he conducted the orchestra. Always available to take the ball, he'd never hide; he had feet like Fred Astaire. 99

John Hughes, *Celtic centre-back of the 1990s, on his team-mates of the time*

" He is the type of player that makes people come to watch football. **"**

Ronald de Boer, *of Glasgow Rangers, on Lubo Moravcik, May 2002*

> **The club could have done much more to help me settle in and feel a part of it.**

Stilian Petrov, *in 2002, recalls arriving at Celtic from CSKA Sofia of Bulgaria as a teenager in 1999*

" I want him to stay around here for the next ten or twelve years. **"**

Martin O'Neill *on Stilian Petrov, November 2002*

A circus act... "

Jock Stein on penalty shoot-outs after Celtic had lost the first one in which they had participated, to be eliminated by Inter Milan at the semi-final stage of the 1972 European Cup

" It saddens me when people remember Dixie only for that. He scored two hat-tricks in cup finals for Celtic, after all. The thing that should be remembered is that Dixie put his hand up and said, "I'll take a penalty." **"**

Bobby Lennox, *2003. Dixie Deans missed from the spot as Celtic lost 5–4 in the semi-final penalty shoot-out to Inter in 1972*

66 To me, that was like getting put out on a technicality. 99

Bobby Lennox, *on losing on penalties to Inter in 1972*

66 Scottish goalkeepers are supposed to be bad enough but an Irish 'keeper in Scotland... I just had to go out and try and prove everyone wrong. **99**

Pat Bonner, *Celtic goalkeeper of the 1980s and 1990s*

66 Everything was done on the cheap – it was murder. The Aberdeen that I left was far better than the Celtic I joined. **99**

Billy McNeill *on his first period as Celtic manager, from 1978 to 1983*

66 Charlie Nicholas was sold behind my back. I still to this day don't know what money they got for Charlie Nicholas. The chairman refused to tell me. 99

Billy McNeill, *in 2002, on Nicholas' departure from Celtic to Arsenal in 1983*

"Animals..." "

Jimmy Johnstone *on the Atletico Madrid team that had three players sent off in the first leg of their European Cup semi-final with Celtic in 1974*

66 He said to me, "What chance have they got of hitting you when you get out there and you start juking and jiving? I can't move, I'm sitting there in that dug-out." **99**

Jimmy Johnstone recalls Jock Stein's words after Johnstone and Stein received death threats prior to Celtic's European Cup semi-final second leg with Atletico in Madrid, 1974

66 Aspects of his game, like decision-making and seeing people in good positions, still have to come but we don't want to lose his natural brilliance in taking people on. If he had it all just now, there would be nothing to look forward to, would there? **99**

Martin O'Neill *on Aiden McGeady, August 2004*

" My main intention is to do what is best for the team by taking on and beating people rather than concerning myself with what will please the fans. If the fans like the way I play the game, that's good but my main motivation is not to be a crowd-pleaser. **"**

Aiden McGeady, *September 2004*

"Not one thin dime..."

Fergus McCann, *a Scots-Canadian, in 1994, on how much he intended to offer the board at Celtic as compensation if they were to relinquish their hold on the club*

66 We have new people, a new plan, a new vision and the strength to go forward. 99

Fergus McCann *on assuming financial control of Celtic and paying off the old board after the club had been on the verge of bankruptcy, 4 March 1994*

66 I caught the beginning of the stadium. I caught just that wind of change and I remember thinking that when this place is full it is going to be quite an arena. I felt the warmth and swell of the Celtic support. **99**

Tony Mowbray, *Celtic centre-back of the 1990s, recalling, in 2004, the opening, in 1995, of the first of the three new stands at today's 60,000-capacity Celtic Park*

“ McCann built a stadium. Oh, what a great, great thing. Ceaucescu built pretty amazing stadiums, so did Mussolini. I'm in it for the team. It's like building La Scala and having a run-of-the-mill pub singer perform. **”**

Jim Kerr, *pop singer, in May 1999, after his consortium's takeover bid for Celtic was turned down by Fergus McCann*

66 My only regret is that the team after the Lions never played long enough because we might have equalled what they had done in Europe. We were getting to semi-finals and we hadn't reached our peak. **99**

David Hay *on Celtic's young players of the early 1970s*

“ I think a lot of people turned up because they wanted to see what people from Albania looked like. **”**

Murdo MacLeod *on the 51,000 crowd that attended Celtic's 1979 European Cup tie with Partizani Tirana, from the then secluded communist state of Albania*

66 When we came out for the match, the noise from the crowd nearly knocked us over. **99**

Willie Buchan, *Celtic's winning goal-scorer, in 2002, on the European record crowd of 146,433 that saw Celtic beat Aberdeen 2–1 in the 1937 Scottish Cup final at Hampden Park*

66 This'll maybe sound blasé but you get used to things like that. You don't even notice the size of the crowd really. I think you'd notice more if there was hardly anybody there. **99**

Bobby Lennox *on playing in front of 110,000 at the Bernabeu Stadium in Celtic's European Cup quarter-final second leg with Real Madrid in March 1980*

66 You think, when travelling to Austria, you are going to a nice, clean, civilised country but my father and sister were in the stand that night and the Rapid fans were pulling their hair and spitting on them. That was Rapid's Nazi squad. **99**

Peter Grant, *in 2003, on the away European Cup-Winners' Cup tie with Rapid Vienna in 1984*

66 I remember Paul McStay saying to Krankl, in very clear English, "You are a cheat." The bottle had landed 20 yards away from their player. 99

Peter Grant, *in 2003, recalls the match with Rapid Vienna at Celtic Park in 1984. The Austrians lost 3–0 but had the match declared void after claiming a bottle had felled Rudi Weinhofer. Hans Krankl was Rapid's captain*

> # " It was almost as if they planned for it. "

David Hay, then Celtic manager, in 1995, on Rapid Vienna's gamesmanship at Celtic Park that led to a third game at neutral Old Trafford, a 1–0 defeat for Celtic, and elimination from the Cup-Winners' Cup

66 We felt that Celtic team could have gone all the way to the final. To lose it on what was ultimately a technicality was sore, especially since we had proved at Celtic Park that we were the better team. **99**

Davie Provan *on the Rapid Vienna fiasco, 2004*

We climbed three mountains and then proceeded to throw ourselves off them.

Billy McNeill, *Celtic manager, after winning 5–4 in a topsy-turvy European Cup-Winners' Cup tie with Partizan Belgrade but going out on away goals on an aggregate 6–6 score, 1989*

66 The hotel was horrendous and we all slept with our clothes on because it was so filthy. The beds were damp and there were no curtains. It is the only trip I've been on where the players were all sitting round a TV at 3am; no-one wanted to go to bed. **99**

Peter Grant *on Celtic's trip to Georgia to play Dynamo Batumi in the European Cup-Winners' Cup in 1995*

66 I was 35 and that is too young for someone to be appointed Celtic manager. 99

David Hay, *speaking in 2002, on becoming Celtic manager in July 1983*

66 One of the directors said,
"If Davie's going to buy a couple of
players the money will have
to come out of his own pocket."
That epitomised their attitude
at that time. **99**

David Hay, *speaking in 1995, on being manager of
Celtic during the 1986–87 season*

> **Davie is too nice to be a football manager.**

Jack McGinn, *Celtic chairman, on recruiting Billy McNeill to replace David Hay as manager, 1987*

❝ When I was at Celtic I was said to be a players' man and maybe that was true. In those days, if the ship was sinking, I would have thrown all 11 lifebelts to the players. Now I would keep one for myself, throw 10 and lose a player. **❞**

David Hay, *Celtic manager from 1983 to 1987, in 1991*

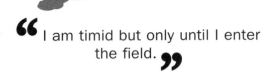

66 I am timid but only until I enter the field. **99**

Juninho, *August 2004*

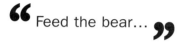

66 Feed the bear... **99**

*Terracing chant for Celtic's all-action, aggressive
midfielder Roy Aitken, 1980s*

❝ They are here to keep their fingers crossed for Celtic, not Henrik Larsson. Henrik Larsson is history. They are here to cheer on the boys on the park. **❞**

Henrik Larsson, *after returning to Celtic Park and scoring in Barcelona's 3–1 Champions League win in September 2004; the Swede received a hostile reception from some Celtic fans*

“ I thought the way he didn't celebrate his goal was great. He scored but he decided to remain quiet about it and we all know why. **”**

Frank Rijkaard, *Barcelona coach, after Henrik Larsson scored Barcelona's third goal in their 3–1 Champions League win at Celtic Park in September 2004, his first appearance at the ground after leaving Celtic in the summer of 2004*

“ Concentration is what makes Stefan Klos such a big player for Rangers and I'd like to get to that level myself. Even when Rangers are leading 2–0 and it's the last minute, Klos has still got that concentration and he's still made saves. I hope I can strive to be like that. **”**

David Marshall, *Celtic goalkeeper, September 2004*

❝ When they attacked we were four players down. **❞**

Tommy Burns on fielding Paolo Di Canio, Pierre van Hooijdonk, Andreas Thom and Jorge Cadete in the same team for a UEFA Cup tie against SV Hamburg in September 1996

" The gaffer says it was men against boys out there. **"**

Garry Flitcroft of Blackburn Rovers passes on a strange claim after Celtic had beaten Blackburn 1–0 in the first leg of their UEFA Cup tie in October 2002. Blackburn's 'gaffer' was ex-Rangers manager Graeme Souness

66 If Celtic score one, we can score three. Hopefully, by 10pm on Thursday, people will be saying, "Bloody hell, that Blackburn are a good team." **99**

Graeme Souness *before Blackburn's 2–0 home defeat to Celtic in the second leg of their UEFA Cup tie, November 2002*

> **"** They should learn a lesson: never talk until the game's finished. **"**

Henrik Larsson, *after the 3–0 UEFA Cup aggregate win over Blackburn Rovers, November 2002*

66 The UEFA Cup is not just one notch up from what we're normally used to; we're talking about four or five notches. **99**

Martin O'Neill, *2003*

66 His heart was ours long before he was offered a peg in the dressing room. He brought with him a fervour and freshness which revealed the real Celtic spirit. **99**

Willie Maley, *Celtic manager, on Jimmy McGrory, Celtic's greatest goal-scorer, 1939*

" A Celtic fan cried, in a pause,
Where Parkhead's fog hung hoary.
We dinna need yer Santa Claus
While we ha'e Jimmy McGrory. **"**

*Poem in the **Sunday Mail**,*
Christmas 1935

" Louie [Macari] left, then myself, then Kenny [Dalglish], and George [Connelly] gave it up. I think if we'd stayed together, we would have sustained a real challenge at the highest level. Deep down, none of us really wanted to leave. "

David Hay, *in 1995, on the break-up of Celtic's talented Quality Street Gang of young players in the 1970s*

“ I was convinced that this boy would be a scorer but I can remember people questioning why I had signed him. **”**

Billy McNeill *on Brian McClair, scorer of 121 goals in 142 games for Celtic between 1983 and 1987*

66 I had more fights with Granty than anybody even though we were on the same team, even though we roomed together. He played for the jersey, even in training games. **99**

Mick McCarthy *on Peter Grant, his Celtic team-mate in the late-1980s*

❝ There's as much chance of McAvennie leaving as there is of us losing 5–1 tomorrow. **❞**

Billy McNeill, *Celtic manager, on 26 August 1988.*
Celtic lost 5–1 to Rangers at Ibrox the following day.
Frank McAvennie was transferred to West Ham

66 I'll finish my career here. I don't want to play for any other club. **99**

Maurice Johnston *at a press conference to announce he would be returning to Celtic from FC Nantes, 12 May 1989*

" Unsporting conduct... "

*FIFA's verdict on fining Maurice Johnston £3,500 for
reneging on his publicly announced agreement to
re-sign for Celtic from Nantes. Instead he joined
Rangers in July 1989*

" A publicity stunt... "

Fergus McCann's *verdict on the appointment of Lou Macari as manager by the Celtic board which McCann was attempting to oust, October 1993*

" HalLoue'en! **"**

Headline in the **Sunday Mail** on 31 October 1993
after Macari had beaten Rangers 2–1 in his first
match as Celtic manager

66 It's a bit like having a dream that you never think is going to become real; the same as becoming a football player here. Then all of a sudden it's reality. Then you get on with the job. **99**

Tommy Burns, *in 1995, on becoming Celtic manager one year previously*

66 I probably did about 15 or 20 years as a manager in those three years. **99**

Tommy Burns, *in 2002, on being Celtic manager, and working with Celtic managing director Fergus McCann, from 1994 to 1997*

66 I felt that a lot of people thought I shouldn't have been there. That's what I was up against from the start. **99**

John Barnes, *speaking in 2002, on being appointed, without any previous experience, head coach at Celtic in June 1999*

" It was just an accident waiting to happen. **"**

John Barnes, in 2002, on the 3–1 home Scottish Cup defeat by First Division Inverness Caledonian Thistle in February 2000 that cost him his job

> **If you put that wee thing out on the park, you'll be done for manslaughter.**

Jimmy Quinn, *Celtic centre-forward, to manager Willie Maley, on first seeing Patsy Gallacher, the 5ft 6in, 7-stone, future Celtic great, 1911*

“ The Mighty Atom **”**

*Celtic supporters' nickname for Patsy Gallacher,
scorer of 196 goals in 464 appearances for Celtic
between 1911 and 1926*

“ I used to sleep with the ball. The first thing I'd do every morning was see if it was there. Football was your outlet. You had nothing else. **”**

Jimmy Johnstone, *in 1995, on growing up in Viewpark, Uddingston*

" The Flying Flea **"**

French journalists' nickname for Jimmy Johnstone
after the European Cup tie with Nantes, 1966

" The wee man would be quiet and then he would do two or three things and we would be two or three up and the other team would be just shattered. "

Evan Williams, *former Celtic goalkeeper, on Jimmy Johnstone, 2003*

66 I don't think he knew what he was going to do next, so what chance did the opposition have? **99**

Tommy Gemmell *on Jimmy Johnstone, 1995*

66 The finest player in Britain. **99**

Jock Stein *on Bobby Murdoch, 1969*

66 He couldn't run and he couldn't jump but by God he could play football. He must have been the best passer of a ball ever to play in the British Isles. **99**

Evan Williams, *in 2003, on former team-mate Bobby Murdoch*

" Och, just let him on the park. **"**

Jock Stein *on being asked how best to use Kenny Dalglish in the team*

" Kenny took some horrific kicks from boys hitting him from the back and what not. You should have seen his legs sometimes. He got a lot of goals that maybe lesser people who weren't as brave as him wouldn't have got. **"**

Jimmy Johnstone, *speaking in 1995, on Kenny Dalglish*

" You could tell that he just didn't like the place, Glasgow, and the pressure of playing for one of the Old Firm sides. You can turn a determined player round but if he hasn't got the determination you can't turn him round. **"**

Liam Brady, *ex-Celtic manager, on striker Tony Cascarino, a record signing at £1.1 million in 1991, who scored four goals in 30 games for the club*

66 Life with the reserves was a sobering experience. At Hamilton, the dressing room was so small that I couldn't stand up without bumping my head on the ceiling but, removed from the hostility and pressures choking me at Parkhead, I began to enjoy myself again. **99**

Tony Cascarino, *in 2000, on finding his level at Celtic*

" It's up to the manager to see where he can best play you but I think I have the skills to play in all positions. **"**

Juninho *on joining Celtic in August 2004*

" The Bhoy from Brazil "

*Slogan on T-shirts on sale in Celtic's superstore the
day after Juninho's debut against Rangers and five
days after he had signed for the club in August 2004*

> **"** It seemed as though everybody else had scored on the night so I would have been disappointed if I hadn't scored. **"**

Aiden McGeady *on getting his first goal at Celtic Park, in the 8–1 victory over Falkirk, September 2004*

66 I don't believe 50,000 fans will travel to Seville. That is madness. It is an exaggeration. I think a fair number will be around 4,000. We are talking about a final to be played on a Wednesday, a day when people normally work. **99**

Rafael Carmona, *security chief at the UEFA Cup final in Seville, May 2003. An estimated 50,000 to 80,000 Celtic fans visited the city for the match*

66 I'd prefer to ask whether the behaviour of the Celtic players was normal in your country. What Balde did to Deco in front of me could have ended his career. There was a lot of commitment in Celtic's game: commitment, toughness and aggression. I'm tempted to use another word – but I won't. 99

José Mourinho, *then Porto coach, answering Martin O'Neill's criticism of his side's gamesmanship in the UEFA Cup final, 21 May 2003*

“ I thought they were great and deserved everything they got. **”**

Paul Lambert *on Porto after the 2003 UEFA Cup final*

" I don't see anything positive about my own performance in the final. Scoring two goals in the final doesn't mean anything if you lose. All I wanted was for Celtic to win the Cup. **"**

Henrik Larsson *after Celtic's 3–2 defeat to Porto in the UEFA Cup final, May 2003*

66 I saw Thommo was going to head the ball back and I gambled – it fell nicely for me. It was mixed emotions. **99**

Henrik Larsson *on intercepting ex-team-mate Alan Thompson's pass-back to score his first Champions League goal for Barcelona, September 2004*

" I've never seen such violence. These dangerous fools got away with hip-high tackles and dirty fouls and I was even punched in the face. We may have lost but I have won a personal victory – I didn't break my legs. A good director could make a great karate film with the Celtic defenders. "

Aruna Dindane, *Anderlecht, after scoring the goal in Anderlecht's 1–0 Champions League victory over Celtic, November 2003*

" I assume the deal might be to do with the bit of improvement we have made on the European scene over the past two years. **"**

Martin O'Neill *on Celtic's proposed £25 million, five-year shirt sponsorship deal with Nike, September 2004*

66 See if you're inside the 18-yard box and you've nobody to stick it to; just stick it in the net. **99**

Jimmy Hogan, *Celtic coach, to his players, 1948*

66 Get the ball on the deck. It won't hurt the grass if we move it about on the deck. **99**

Jimmy Hogan, *1948*

> 66 I thought he felt a bit inferior at that time because he had been playing non-League down in Wales and now here he was at Celtic – but what a lift that must have been for his confidence. 99

Alec Boden, *in 2002, on Jock Stein joining Celtic as a centre-half from Llanelli in December 1951*

“ The only time I know is seven past Niven. **”**

Charlie Tully *after Celtic had won 7–1 in the League Cup final against Rangers, whose goalkeeper was George Niven, 19 October 1957*

66 Martin seems to have the ability to feel what is going to happen and to feel when he has to change things. He maybe makes a mistake one time in ten; the other nine times he is right. **99**

Lubo Moravcik *on O'Neill's managerial abilities, May 2002*

66 Martin did have one thing going for him when he arrived up there in Glasgow – he didn't need to work too hard to get fans to come to the ground. All he had to do was tell them it's a Saturday! What a luxury, massive home crowds virtually guaranteed. **99**

Brian Clough *on his former player turned manager Martin O'Neill, 2002*

❝ I read some headlines saying that we were after some Bulgarian player. If our scout was out watching a game in Estonia where he was playing, when I was sending him somewhere else? I'm going to sack him! **❞**

Martin O'Neill reflects on newspaper transfer speculation, April 2003

❝ What else can I say? How many times can I say it? How many times do you want to ask the same thing? How many times do you want to be wrong? **❞**

*Celtic manager **Martin O'Neill** beats off the latest story linking him to a club in the FA Premiership after being linked with the Spurs job, October 2003*

66 My teams would lose games where it became a scrap. Martin always wins. **99**

Liam Brady, *in April 2002, compares his management of Celtic to that of Martin O'Neill*

66 Get tight, shut down, don't let anyone shoot. That's what the manager wants and we preach it on the training pitch. **99**

Steve Walford, *coach at Celtic under manager Martin O'Neill, August 2004*

66 The manager has instilled an unbelievable air of confidence in us. He makes you play better and he makes you want to win. He's got an awful will to win and he has really transmitted that to the players. **99**

Paul Lambert *after Celtic's 6–2 victory over Rangers in Martin O'Neill's first Old Firm match as Celtic manager, August 2000*

66 He is a strong guy and he knows what he wants to do in every game. He has been very strong in situations at crucial moments. He really is the boss. **99**

Lubo Moravcik *on Martin O'Neill, May 2002*

" The Celtic supporters were out of this world. I've still to find supporters to better them. **"**

Tommy Gemmell, *1995*

❝ I've seen some dire games in England. You keep giving yourselves too many pats on the back, saying you have the best league in the world. **❞**

Gordon Strachan

66 I have never worked with a technically better player than Nakamura. For sublime touch and vision there has been none better in my career. **99**

Gordon Strachan *on Shunsuke Nakamura, the Japan international, whom he signed from Perugia in 2005*

66 I don't believe it. There must be a rule that says we don't go through. I will wake up tomorrow and find someone has scored an extra goal against us somewhere. I better check Teletext tomorrow to make sure. 99

Gordon Strachan, *after the 1–0 win over Manchester United took the Hoops into the Champions League knockout phase*

" I made the decision in seconds. This is a chance I just couldn't turn down. I'm proud to be asked to follow Martin O'Neill and I'm looking forward to the challenge with a world famous club. "

Gordon Strachan, *on his appointment at Celtic Park, May 2005*

It has been an honour and privilege to have served the club and its supporters during that time and be part of Celtic history.

Martin O'Neill *leaves Celtic to spend time with his sick wife, May 2005*

66 To win by 20 points is scary. **99**

Gordon Strachan *sees Celtic coast to the*
title in his first season

66 We are the only club in the history of football who can be the champions by 20 points and be under pressure in the first game of the season. **99**

Strachan *reflects on the pressures of managing Celtic*

" I have had seven great years here but I know what I have to do now. I'm a Barcelona player. It felt good but it was very difficult to celebrate when I had such a great time here. **"**

Henrik Larsson *has mixed feelings about scoring for Barcelona against Celtic, September 2004*

66 [Gary] Neville came over and said, "I think he'll miss it – his head's gone down". **99**

Neil Lennon *reveals the Manchester United skipper predicted Louis Saha's Champions League penalty miss at Celtic Park*

" He is a genius. I don't know what more he can do apart from carrying the players on his shoulders and playing at the same time. **"**

Gordon Strachan *admires the contribution of Shunsuke Nakamura*

> **"** He's got black hair,
> He plays with flair,
> He leaves them for dead
> When he uses his left peg.
>
> He's our Rising son
> When he scores for fun.
> He's our NAKAMURA
> He'll be our top scorer. **"**

*Lyrics for a Nakamura song, from fan site
www.kerrydalestreet.co.uk*

66 I've never hidden the fact that I'm a Celtic supporter, so you can imagine what this means to me. **99**

Paul Hartley *completes his dream move from Hearts in January 2007*

" My dad said when Celtic first came in for me that I should pick them. He said he wanted to see me play there. I took him to Celtic Park for an Old Firm game when I was at Everton. He filmed the fans when they sang "You'll Never Walk Alone". He still has it on his computer at home in Denmark. **"**

Thomas Gravesen *explains why he moved to Celtic from Real Madrid*

66 I'm just glad I managed to get out of Nacho Novo's pocket to collect these awards. **99**

Aiden McGeady, *Celtic winger, on receiving his Player of the Year and Young Player of the Year awards in April 2008. Novo, the Rangers player, had suggested he'd had McGeady in his pocket in the Old Firm encounter four days earlier*

66 Champions League nights
are so special at Celtic Park.
They are occasions I will
never forget. **99**

Jan Vennegoor of Hesselink, *Celtic player from
2006 to 2009*

" I had a day off and wanted to help a sick child. One kid wrote a letter to a TV station. They let me know that he really liked me as a player and asked if I could meet him. I flew to Poland in the morning with my club jersey and returned that night. I will always help somebody if I have the chance. **"**

Artur Boruc *shows he is one of the good guys*

First can be nowhere here.

Gordon Strachan, *Celtic manager, jokes, in 2007, about the pressures related to being in charge of an Old Firm club*

66 We have no chance of winning the Champions League. Give me £40,000,000 and I might change my mind. **99**

Gordon Strachan, *Celtic manager, under pressure in 2007 for his decision-making in Champions League matches, stresses how Celtic's lack of serious financial clout hampers the club in modern European football*

66 I liked the way Celtic played against us. They played with their hearts. You never know, a team such as that could triumph. Look at Porto in 2004. It was a simple team. If you believe in your own capabilities and remain humble, surprises are always possible. **99**

Clarence Seedorf, *Milan midfield player, talks up Celtic's Champions League-winning chances after their victory over the Italian club in November 2007*

66 I just don't shake hands with people I don't like. I just don't like the way Rangers players play football – especially Barry Ferguson. We lost a fight, not a football match – I didn't see much football in this battle. We were just kicked all day and that's it. **99**

Artur Boruc, *Celtic's Poland international goalkeeper, on refusing to shake the hands of his opponents after a tempestuous Old Firm derby at Ibrox in autumn 2007*

66 Celtic need Rangers. Rangers need Celtic. Maybe some supporters hate each other, but they love each other too because they need the derby. If there was no derby something would be missing. **99**

Andreas Hinkel, *Celtic's Germany international full-back, offers his point of view on the Old Firm rivalry*

" You people sometimes are like those serial killers you see in films who send out these horrible messages: the serial killer who cuts out the words, 'I am going to get you' or 'Your wife is next'. You are the very same. **"**

Gordon Strachan, *Celtic manager, reacting vehemently to the Scottish football media, expressing his belief that he had been deliberately misquoted in the press*

66 If you can spend four years as the Glasgow Celtic manager, you can be the Prime Minister with ease. **99**

Gordon Strachan, *Celtic manager from 2005 to 2009, on the demands of the job*

" I think we should be playing in a bigger and more competitive League. I think we'd be a bigger football club and a better football club. I think that's a position that's rightfully Celtic's. "

Dermot Desmond, *Celtic's major shareholder, 2008*

> **I believe Celtic and Rangers have to keep the Scottish League alive. That's why they have to stay here.**

Arsène Wenger, *Arsenal manager, contributes to the ongoing debate about the Old Firm clubs leaving Scottish football, after a Champions League qualifying match at Celtic Park in August 2009*

“ I'm not going to pretend I didn't think about it. I'm a Celtic fan. It's where I'm from, a big part of who I am, and, of course, there's the chance of Champions League football. But then I looked at what we had built at Burnley and I knew I had to stay and carry on this incredible adventure. **”**

Owen Coyle, *in late July 2009, explains why he turned down the chance to become Celtic manager that summer*

66 It's a striving for a type of Utopia: to have the best team that you can get, with every position filled with high-quality footballers, even if you never actually get there. 99

Tony Mowbray, *newly appointed as Celtic manager, outlines his aims, August 2009*

❝ I know that my team is in for a difficult night – but so are Utrecht **❞**

Neil Lennon, *Celtic-manager, prior to the Europa League play-off round second leg against the Dutch club. Trailing 2–0 after the game at Celtic Park, Utrecht eased to a 4–0 home victory on the night, and a place in the group stage*

66 Player trading is going to be a bigger part of our future. We will try to buy low and sell high after getting some good years' service from players. **99**

Peter Lawwell, *Celtic chief executive, tells it like it is as Celtic enter the second decade of the 21st century*

" Something happens to me when Celtic run on to the park... for me that is the highlight. I'd show up just for that. Those hoops... I love the clean green and white. Not only do they represent me but I feel well represented by them. My heart just sings a song when I see them running out. **"**

Billy Connolly